GAME DAY

Get Ready for a Gymnastics Meet

by: Emma Huddleston

Consultant: Beth Gambro
Reading Specialist, Yorkville, Illinois

Minneapolis, Minnesota

Teaching Tips

Before Reading

- Look at the cover of the book. Discuss the picture and the title.

- Ask readers to brainstorm a list of what they already know about gymnastics meets. What can they expect to see in this book?

- Go on a picture walk, looking through the pictures to discuss vocabulary and make predictions about the text.

During Reading

- Read for purpose. Encourage readers to think about preparing for a gymnastics meet as they are reading.

- Ask readers to look for the details of the book. What needs to happen before the big meet?

- If readers encounter an unknown word, ask them to look at the sounds in the word. Then, ask them to look at the rest of the page. Are there any clues to help them understand?

After Reading

- Encourage readers to pick a buddy and reread the book together.

- Ask readers to name two things from the book that a gymnast does to get ready for a meet. Find the pages that tell about these things.

- Ask readers to write or draw something they learned about gymnastics.

Credits:
Cover and title page, © PeopleImages/iStock and © RichLegg/iStock; 3, © mg7/iStock; 5, © vgajic/iStock; 7, © FatCamera/iStock; 8-9, © Master1305/Shutterstock; 11, © SolStock/iStock; 13, © FG Trade/iStock; 15, © t:M_a_y_a/iStock; 16-17, © Rawpixel.com/Shutterstock; 19, © kali9/iStock; 21, © ssj414/iStock; 22TL,© Polhansen/iStock; 22TM, © CasarsaGuru/iStock; 22TR, © Buenafoto/iStock; 22BL, © versh/Shutterstock; 22BR,© nazarethman/iStock; 23TL, © kali9/iStock; 23TM, © Tuned_In/iStock; 23TR, © mg7/iStock; 23BL, © Juan Jose Napuri/iStock; 23BM, © bmcent1/iStock; and 23BR, © brusinski/iStock.

Library of Congress Cataloging-in-Publication Data

Names: Huddleston, Emma, author.
Title: Get ready for a gymnastics meet / by Emma Huddleston.
Description: Minneapolis, Minnesota : Bearport Publishing Company, [2024] |
  Series: Game day | Includes bibliographical references and index.
Identifiers: LCCN 2023002707 (print) | LCCN 2023002708 (ebook) | ISBN
  9798888220580 (library binding) | ISBN 9798888222546 (paperback) | ISBN
  9798888223734 (ebook)
Subjects: LCSH: Gymnastics--Juvenile literature. | Gymnasts--Juvenile
  literature.
Classification: LCC GV461.3 .H83 2024 (print) | LCC GV461.3 (ebook) | DDC
  796.44--dc23/eng/20230126
LC record available at https://lccn.loc.gov/2023002707
LC ebook record available at https://lccn.loc.gov/2023002708

Copyright © 2024 Bearport Publishing Company. All rights reserved. No part of this publication may be reproduced in whole or in part, stored in any retrieval system, or transmitted in any form or by any means, electronic, mechanical, photocopying, recording, or otherwise, without written permission from the publisher.

For more information, write to Bearport Publishing, 5357 Penn Avenue South, Minneapolis, MN 55419.

Contents

Flying High 4

All about Gymnastics 22

Glossary 23

Index 24

Read More 24

Learn More Online 24

About the Author 24

Flying High

I put my hands on the mat.

Then, I push off.

I spin in the air and land with a smile.

Tomorrow is the day of my gymnastics **meet**.

I am ready!

My **coach** helps me **stretch**.

I do my tricks over and over.

Say gymnastics like jim-NAS-tiks

Trying a new flip can be scary.

But my coach tells me I can do it.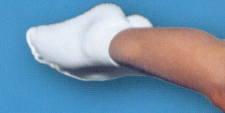

I am brave.

Look what I can do now!

Later, I eat dinner with my family.

A good meal gives me **energy**.

My body needs different kinds of food to stay strong.

After dinner, I go to bed early.

I want lots of rest before the big day.

I dream of my meet.

When I wake up, I put on my **leotard**.

It is red with black.

Then, I tie up my hair.

I need to be able to see well.

At the gym, I stretch with my team.

We run and **tumble** to warm up.

The gym is busy as the meet starts.

People watch and clap.

I cheer while I wait for my turn.

Then, I am up on the beam.

It is time to show off my hard work.

I love gymnastics!

All about Gymnastics

There are many different events in gymnastics.

Balance beam

Floor

Parallel bars

Uneven bars

Vault

Glossary

coach the person who teaches and leads a sports team

energy the power needed to move and do things

leotard a tight piece of clothing worn for gymnastics

meet a gathering for a sporting event

stretch to move the body in a way that pulls muscles longer

tumble to turn, twist, and flip in gymnastics

Index

coach 6, 8
dinner 10, 12
leotard 14–15
meet 6, 12, 18
rest 12
stretch 6, 16
team 16
tumble 16

Read More

Leed, Percy. *Gymnastics: A First Look (Read about Sports)*. Minneapolis: Lerner Publications, 2023.

Rose, Rachel. *Simone Biles: Gymnastics Superstar (Bearcub Bios)*. Minneapolis: Bearport Publishing Company, 2023.

Learn More Online

1. Go to **www.factsurfer.com** or scan the QR code below.
2. Enter **"Gymnastics Meet"** into the search box.
3. Click on the cover of this book to see a list of websites.

About the Author

Emma Huddleston lives in St. Paul with her family. She enjoys playing sports and did gymnastics when she was young, too!